BIRMINGHAM THEN & NOW

MARK NORTON

The History Press

First published 2010

The History Press
The Mill, Brimscombe Port
Stroud, Gloucestershire, GL5 2QG
www.thehistorypress.co.uk

British Library Cataloguing in Publication Data.
A catalogue record for this book is available from the British Library.

ISBN 978 0 7524 5722 2

Typesetting and origination by The History Press
Printed in Malta
Manufacturing managed by Jellyfish Print Solutions Ltd

CONTENTS

ST GEORGE'S CHURCH at the corner of Tower Street and Great Russell Street undergoing demolition in the early 1960s as the area was being redeveloped as Newtown. Great Russell Street disappeared from maps of the city at this time and is now just a memory. St George's Park marks the site of the church and some old gravestones are still in place today.

ACKNOWLEDGEMENTS

A book like this is not possible without a good selection of 'then' pictures. Three of them are from my own collection and were taken by my late father, Dennis. They feature on pages 26, 49, and 76-77. I am very grateful to Bill Stace for allowing the use of pictures taken by his late father, Leonard. These feature on pages 11-12, 29-31, 34-36, 39 and 41 (as well as the back and front covers). I thank the Trinity Mirror Group for their permission to reproduce the picture on page 66. The remaining pictures in the book come from an archive owned by Geoff Thompson. Geoff worked for the Planning Department of Birmingham City Council and was able to acquire the slides following an office move in the 1990s. I am extremely grateful to Geoff for allowing the use of pictures from his archive in this book.

For their assistance with caption information or 'now' views I thank Mark Barrett, Andy Doherty, Wilfred Hastings, Geoff Johnson and Giri Reddy. I also thank my proof-readers, Radha Reddy and my wife, Claire.

The internet has proved to be a great source of research material for this book and I would especially like to mention the following websites: www.birmingham.gov.uk, www.british-history.ac.uk, en.wikipedia.org, billdargue.jimdo.com, www.astonbrook-through-astonmanor.co.uk and www.oldladywood.co.uk.

INTRODUCTION

As someone who grew up in 1970s Birmingham, it is not surprising that I failed to appreciate the history of the city during my early years. The drab, concrete buildings that filled the city centre did little to create a sense of civic pride or to inspire me to understand the past. It was only the realisation of the importance of photographs of the city taken by my father before the Inner Ring Road was constructed that finally made me appreciate that Birmingham was a city with a fascinating history.

My first book, *Birmingham Past & Present: In My Father's Footsteps*, was filled with my father's photographs. Research undertaken for that book sparked an interest that has grown and grown. Through my efforts to share this interest with others I have been given access to amazing photographic archives. It is thanks to the kindness of Geoff Thompson and Bill Stace, the owners of these archives, that this book has been made possible.

What I find amazing about Birmingham is the scale of the projects that are undertaken. This immense scale is well illustrated in Chapter 1 and especially Chapter 4. The breathtaking visions of a better future have no doubt been inspired by the city motto, 'Forward', but there is little doubt that some of these visions were flawed and time has proven that many of the changes undertaken were misguided. As a result, many will look back at what was lost and wonder, 'Was it worth it?' The pictures in this book will help you make your own mind up.

Many of the 'Then' pictures in this book were unlabelled and undated. Some were easy to identify but many required extensive research. This involved cross-referencing with other pictures in the collection or published elsewhere, reference to aerial photos and study of reprints of old maps. I am very confident about the outcome of this research but, since Birmingham has changed so dramatically, the reader must trust me when viewing some of the 'Now' pictures! Errors are possible and I welcome any feedback and comments via the publisher.

A recurring theme during the period of research undertaken for this book was how Birmingham continues to change and evolve. Early plans

AN AERIAL VIEW of the area around the Bullring, *c.* 1964. To the top left is Moor Street Station while New Street Station is visible at the bottom and is not yet affected by redevelopment. The Rotunda is almost complete, as is Manzoni Gardens in the centre of the picture. The grand vision of a modern city is clearly visible from this elevated viewpoint.

for rebuilding the whole area within Paradise Circus were announced, making the loss of what was there before seem even more pointless. Work on the rebuilding of New Street Station commenced, as did work on the new library. Finally, several tower blocks, including Lapworth House, were demolished as the Highgate area once again saw a phase of regeneration commence. It seems that Birmingham is a city that can never stand still – it can only move forward.

1

BULLRING AND MARKETS AREA

MOST LIKELY DATING from the very early years of the 1960s, this view of the proposed design for the Bullring Shopping Centre is very close to the finished product that opened in 1964. The way the artist has made the old parts of the city look grey and depressing while the future city is clean, bright and colourful was no doubt deliberate!

It is often said the Bullring (as the modern-day marketeers would have us call it) is the heart of Birmingham. If that is so, then it reflects the health of the nation well, as this heart has undergone major surgery twice in a period of less than forty years. In the early 1960s it was the creation of the groundbreaking, but ultimately unsuccessful, Bull Ring Shopping Centre. At the start of the twenty-first century it was the coming of the Bullring, a shopping complex to rival any other – and one that has become an asset to the city rather than an embarrassment.

Of course, there is more to the Bullring than just shopping. The surrounding area has a long history of being the home of markets of all kind dating back to 1166 and the granting of a charter to hold a market by King Henry II. In the 1950s there was the Fish Market on the corner of Spiceal Street and Bell Lane, Smithfield Fruit and Vegetable Wholesale Market in Moat Lane and the Wholesale Meat Market in Bradford Street. Those that survived the building of the Bull Ring Shopping Centre would ultimately disappear during another period of redevelopment in the 1970s and the creation of Birmingham Wholesale Markets. At the same time as Bull Ring was being built, the Indoor and Rag Markets would find themselves being torn down and rebuilt too. What was sadly lost under the eastern side of Bullring was the Outdoor Market, a place full of real characters. Whatever your age, and whatever your feelings about the Bullring over the last fifty years, the pictures that follow will no doubt stir many a memory.

THE REAR OF the impressive Market Hall as it was in the mid-1950s. The street sign to the left says Worcester Street (which survives today in a much reduced form having been downgraded to a service road near the Rotunda). The Market Hall was completed in 1835 and was designed by Charles Edge. Charles would go on to complete the Town Hall after the original architects went bust. Despite the loss of its roof during the bombing raids on Birmingham in August 1940, it continued to serve as a market as major redevelopment went on around it. In 2010 the area is still dedicated to shopping as the West Mall of Bullring now occupies the site.

CLEARLY ILLUSTRATING HOW the Market Hall (visible to the far left of the picture above) was surrounded by development as it saw out its final years, here we see the result of demolition work of the buildings of the long-gone Bell Street. Modernity is taking over the city as St Martin's House nears completion and space-age lamp-posts mark the site of St Martin's Circus. Of most interest is the siting of the statue of Nelson: having been removed from his position outside the front of the Market Hall in September 1959, he would remain at this temporary site until his home near the new Outdoor Market was ready in November 1961. Today, Bullring West Mall extends to cover this area too and the statue of Nelson stands nearby.

THE FRONT OF the Market Hall featured two massive Doric columns either side of the entrance which made for a very grand appearance. Perhaps surprisingly, the shops to either side were part of the original design and not added later as it may appear. The picture above dates from around 1960 and contrasts with the view from 2010 showing shops and restaurants near to the entrance of the Bullring West Mall (where the entrance to the old Market Hall used to stand). Today's shopping temples are no longer adorned with the architectural features of ancient Greece!

THIS VIEW OF the Bull Ring from mid-1959 shows the early stages of redevelopment in the area. The statue of Nelson is yet to be moved and Midland Red buses still drop off passengers outside St Martin's church and the Woolworths store. But times are changing, and the concrete that will change the face of the city is being mixed and poured to form the new Bullring Outdoor Market and the Inner Ring Road. The Fish Market that stood on the corner of Bell Street and Spiceal Street has been demolished. In 2010 it is St Martin's church that helps tie these scenes together.

BY MID-1961 the car park at the corner of Park Street and Bullring provided an excellent vantage point for witnessing the remodeling of this part of the city. The road system is progressing apace and the area being created for the Outdoor Market is starting to take shape. The site at the upper right of the picture would later become the home of the Rotunda, a dramatic contrast to the old Market Hall. The 2010 view is also from a car park in Park Street – but, given the city's desire to knock down and rebuild, this is a completely different car park than that of 1961. The Bullring East Mall and the Selfridges' building obscure much of the view, but a small part of St Martin's church is just visible to the far left of both pictures.

MOST LIKELY DATING from late 1958, the picture above shows the area of Moor Street that was demolished to make way for the Outdoor Market and Inner Ring Road. Indeed, in the window of William Hughes is a sign that says, 'Moving Shortly to 64 Dale End', while the unidentified shop to the far right is more explicit, with a sign proclaiming, 'Owing to Ring Road Development we are moving to…'. To the very far-left part the frontage of the Woolworths store can be seen and provides a good link with the pictures on the preceding pages. In 2010 this area is covered by Bullring East Mall but at least Moor Street News continues the tradition of shops fronting onto this historic street.

THE OUTDOOR MARKET in around 1970 – most likely on a winter's day, given the thick overcoats being worn. This conveys the image of Birmingham that proved difficult to shake off: an image of cars, vans and buses flying overhead as the citizens were forced to walk through concrete passageways. Only via the wholesale demolition of the area has this image been improved and site of the market is now part of Bullring East Mall. To the right of the lamp-post is the statue of Nelson and a child's roundabout ride. Although not a nice place to sit and eat fish and chips from the nearby Jolly Fryer, it was very popular! The large sign for Co-Operative Shopping is a reminder of the Co-Op store that was a feature of High Street for many years before being replaced by the Pavilions Shopping Centre.

THE ENTRANCE TO the Bull Ring Shopping Centre and the Indoor Market, *c.* 1970. To the upper right the sign for F.W. Woolworths shows that the company built a new store close to site of the old one on Spiceal Street and it was, for many years, the flagship store of the Bull Ring. Out of view to the left is St Martin's church. In 2010 all traces of the Bull Ring Shopping Centre have disappeared under Bullring West Mall.

WHEN THE OLD Market Hall was finally demolished at the end of 1963, Manzoni Gardens were created in its place and above we see the scene, *c.* 1970. The gardens were named after Sir Herbert Manzoni, who was the city engineer during the building of the Inner Ring Road and who was instrumental in seeing the project get off the drawing board and through to completion. For many years it was a nice place to sit and relax, despite being surrounded by a busy road on three sides. However, as the years passed it became more rundown and tatty, and it started to attract drunks; you were less likely to find old ladies sitting alone as seen in 1970. Manzoni Gardens were swallowed up by Bullring West Mall.

THIS IMAGE OF the Rotunda and the famous fibreglass bull that adorned the Bull Ring Shopping Centre is a superb representation of 1960s Birmingham. Taken from Smallbrook Queensway, it shows the Rotunda not long after completion in 1965 (as it is clear from the fact that only one floor is occupied). The Rotunda was Grade II listed in 2000 and later underwent a conversion from office space to apartments that was completed in 2008. The view from 2010 shows the changes made to the exterior, especially the addition of larger windows, to create a more comfortable living environment.

WITH THE LOSS of the old stops near St Martin's Church, Midland Red needed somewhere else for their buses to go. The development of the Bull Ring Shopping Centre provided an ideal opportunity for the creation of a new bus station and this c. 1964 picture shows the entrance off Dudley Street. It was possible to exit the bus station and walk directly into the indoor market or access the Bull Ring via an escalator. During the building of the new Bullring, the disused bus station became the temporary home of the Indoor Market until the new market building on Edgbaston Street was completed in September 2000. In 2010 the bus station has become the service yard for Bullring Link stores.

MIDLAND RED BUSES brought many people from outside of Birmingham into the city centre, a service that the corporation buses could not provide. The company operated from 1904 (originally named the Birmingham & Midland Motor Omnibus Co.) until the years of bus deregulation in the 1980s when it was split up. Today, First Midland Red run the 144 service with vehicles painted in the corporate First livery so the famous red buses no longer ply the streets of Birmingham. Above we see a 144 at the new terminus in Smallbrook Queensway, just a stone's throw from the old bus station. The service dates back to 1928. Until 1976 it carried passengers all the way from Birmingham to Malvern but in 2010 it only goes as far as Worcester.

Below is the interior of the old bus station. Although intended to get passengers quickly and easily to the new shopping facilities it was not a nice place to wait, and was full of choking diesel fumes – so you also took your life in your hands trying to cross from the stops to the safety of the shops!

SMITHFIELD MARKET OCCUPIED a huge site to the south of St Martin's church. Dating back to 1817, the Wholesale Fruit and Vegetable Market seen above was added in 1883. This lively scene captures the essence of market life and provides a view of the grandeur of the building. Smithfield Market was demolished following the creation of the Birmingham Wholesale Markets Precinct in 1974.

SMITHFIELD HOUSE ON the corner of Moat Lane and Digbeth provides a link with the past and the historic market site by virtue of its name. In the above image, from around 1969, the market building can be seen to the left of Smithfield House. In 2010, the replacement Wholesale Markets can be seen instead.

THE CITY MEAT Market was located close to Smithfield Market in nearby Bradford Street. Having been built in 1897, it suffered the same fate as Smithfield in that it was replaced by the new Wholesale Markets and was demolished in the mid-1970s. The picture above shows the interior of the market at the end of another busy day of trading. In 2010 the site of the market building is of little architectural interest!

2

CITY CENTRE TO FIVE WAYS

AN ATTRACTIVE DISPLAY of Christmas lights, *c.* 1966. The view is looking up New Street from close to the Odeon cinema. The hotel to the left of the Odeon was the Arden.

WHAT BETTER PLACE to start a walk through the city centre than New Street Station? This August 1964 picture was taken in the southern half of the station, the part that was originally built for the Midland Railway and opened in 1885. The view is from platform eight looking westwards with platform seven to the right. The curved cast-iron roof lets light stream down to the platforms, something unknown in the station of today.

The footbridge that connected the platforms was also a public right of way through the station and this meant that tickets could not be checked on entry and exit. Instead, the task had to be performed on the train at approaching stations such as Five Ways. The 1960s redevelopment of New Street has proved unpopular and the station is already being reworked as part of a project known as the Birmingham Gateway, due to be completed by 2015.

THE NAME OF Stafford Street had been a feature of maps of Birmingham since at least 1731 but the Inner Ring Road development would put an end to that. This picture from around 1963 shows a very grubby and rundown street, but business goes on (despite the plans to replace these shops with James Watt Queensway seen in the view from 2010 below).

THIS VERY GRAND late Victorian building on the corner of Dale End, to the left, and James Watt Street, to the right, had originally been a hotel known as The Bell Tavern. In this picture from around 1963 it is the premises of David J. Hill, who supplied bar fittings so a link with beer industry remained. An interesting feature to the left of the shop entrance is an old blue police post. In 2010 James Watt Street has been curtailed near its junction with Corporation Street due to the construction of the Queen Elizabeth II Law Courts, the rear of which is seen below.

A VIEW OF New Street from close to the site of the Odeon cinema, c. 1957. At the time the city centre was a confusing array of one-way streets and that clearly affected New Street as all the vehicles are facing away from the camera. To the right of the Midland Red bus is the entrance to Corporation Street and the large white building in the centre was, at the time, the Marshall & Snellgrove department store. In 2010 the whole area is pedestrianised and the Marshall & Snellgrove store is now the Britannia Hotel.

NOW LOOKING THE opposite way down New Street from close to the junction with Stephenson Place, the street sign in the centre reinforces the point that navigating the city centre by car was far from simple! The Burton menswear store occupies the lower floor of Princes Corner (which marks the start of Corporation Street, the grand shopping street promoted by Joseph Chamberlain in the 1870s and forged through an area formerly occupied by streets of slums). The Marshall & Snellgrove store is prominent in the centre of the picture. The scene in 2010 is remarkably similar but the car is now banished from the area.

STEPHENSON STREET, LOOKING towards Stephenson Place (with the junction with Lower Temple Street to the left), *c.* 1960. In the centre is the Gothic Exchange building erected in 1865 and torn down 100 years later. The cars to the right are parked outside the Queens Hotel; Queens was opened at the same time as the original New Street Station in 1854 and demolished in 1966. It is a small relief that the Midland Hotel and adjoining shops, seen on the left, survive in 2010. If plans proceed, this may in the future become the site of the Midland Metro terminus, relocated from Snow Hill.

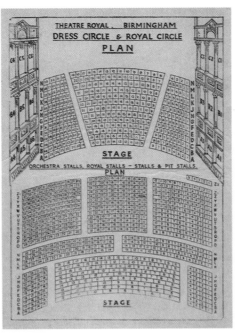

THERE HAD BEEN a Theatre Royal on New Street since the 1770s and this Theatre Royal (seen here in the midst of demolition in around 1957) had been standing since 1902. It was very popular with the people of Birmingham and its loss was keenly felt by many; its demise came about via a combination of an expired lease, the need for Woolworths to find a new store while the Bullring was being rebuilt and the commercial desires of one Jack Cotton. The picture shows the theatre from the rear as viewed from Stephenson Street. The seat plan featured on the small envelope that tickets were placed in when purchased. Woolworths departed the store long before the demise of the chain as a whole and the 2010 picture, taken from roughly the same location as the demolition scene above, shows that the lower floors are now a gym.

THE JUNCTION OF New Street and Ethel Street shows the Woolworths store that replaced the Theatre Royal nearing completion. This would indicate a date of around 1963. The fine, Victorian building that ran down the east side of Ethel Street was nearing the end of its life. All the shops are closed and the upper floors, which once housed the Colonnade Hotel and later the Chamber of Commerce, lie empty and unused. What a shame that the scene in 2010 reveals an example of 1960s architecture that has dated far less well than what was lost from this site.

THE TOP END of New Street, *c.* 1959. It is reassuring to see so much still in place in 2010. However, it would not be so without the effort of conservationists. As late as 1974 the old General Post Office, built in 1891 and seen to the left of the picture, was threatened with demolition but was saved thanks to the efforts of The Victorian Society. Today it serves as office space. To the right is the Town Hall, originally opened in 1834. It reopened in October 2007 after a long and protracted refurbishment costing £34 million and is now a superb venue for concerts and other performances. In between these survivors is the Midland Institute that is sadly no more. More of this building can be seen later on.

THE AREA THAT is today occupied by Victoria Square and the famous 'Floozie in the Jacuzzi' was once the site of Christ Church. Built in 1805 and demolished in 1899 it was replaced by shops and offices but Christ Church Passage provides a reminder of its existence. The passage provides a short cut from New Street to Waterloo Street – and the early 1960s picture shows that it was well used. With the demolition of the shops in the early 1970s the name 'passage' became something of a misnomer but, as the 2010 picture shows, the steps are still in place and little changed.

THIS MISTY VIEW down Hill Street in around 1959 clearly shows the bridge link that connected the General Post Office to the left with the parcels office to the right. Under the bridge, the building in the centre was the Golden Eagle public house that was demolished to make way for a small car park. In 2010 the area at the bottom of Hill Street has changed dramatically with the creation of the Orion Building and Beetham Tower.

A VERY ATTRACTIVE view of Victoria Square dating from the early 1970s. The statue of Victoria is a bronze copy of the original marble one that was erected in 1901. The grassed area was the site of shops that were demolished a couple of years before this picture was taken and the steps seen to the right of centre are Christ Church Passage. The original plan for the Inner Ring Road submitted to Parliament in 1946 included a roundabout on this site and many buildings on the south side of Colmore Row would have been demolished to accommodate the dual carriageway that was also planned. In 2010 Victoria Square is a highlight of the city centre with the famous statue by Dhruva Mistry taking centre stage.

THE CROSSROADS AT the junction of Hill Street and Navigation Street. Given the state of construction of the Rotunda, this picture most likely dates from late 1963. On the far left is the rear of the Queens Hotel in Stephenson Street. In the centre is one of the entrances to New Street Station, this one being the western end of Queens Drive. In the distance is the spire of St Martin's Church. A poster to the right advertises the 'City of Birmingham Holiday Express', which offered a visit to a different resort each day, bringing you home each night. It is hard to miss TED'S 'OTDOGS in the foreground! In 2010 the Rotunda provides the common link in an otherwise unrecognisable scene.

A VIEW OF Paradise Street, *c*. 1959. The clue to the dating of this picture comes from the building covered in scaffolding in the centre of the view: it was one of the first modern buildings erected in this part of the city and, in 2010, it is once again covered with scaffolding as refurbishment takes place. To the left, behind the bus, is the Royal Mail parcels office at the top of Hill Street which was demolished in 1975. Behind the 'TURN LEFT' sign is the terracotta frontage of Queen's College, now Queen's Chambers.

A VISIT TO Birmingham by the Queen and Prince Philip. This picture most likely dates from 24 May 1963, when they visited the Bullring almost a year before it would be officially opened by the Prince. The road sign to the left says Ratcliff Place and this was the home of the Midland Institute and Central Library seen on the following pages. The buildings to the right were Christ Church buildings but the section visible was more commonly known as Galloway's Corner due to the presence of a chemist and camera shop called Galloway's. An interesting question about this picture might be 'why is the Ugandan flag flying from the Town Hall?!' In 2010, with Galloway's Corner having been demolished in around 1971, buildings in Waterloo Street can now be seen to the right of the Town Hall.

THIS STATUE OF James Watt stood at the entrance to Ratcliff Place from 1868 until wholesale development of this area for the creation of Paradise Circus resulted in the statue being removed. In 2010 it stands outside the Central Library (officially opened by Harold Wilson, MP in January 1974). With this building failing to achieve listed status in 2009, it is almost inevitable that the statue will be on the move once again. The new £193 million library being constructed on Centenary Square between the Birmingham Repertory Theatre and Baskerville House is due to open in 2013.

THE TRULY SPLENDID premises of the Birmingham & Midland Institute, pictured shortly before demolition, *c.* 1965. The building curving round from Paradise Street into Ratcliff Place was opened in 1857. So successful was the institute in its aims to educate both the working and the middle classes that the Gothic extension, seen on the left, was opened in Paradise Street in 1881. It is nice to know that the Birmingham & Midland Institute survives as a charitable organisation to this day, operating out of

attractive premises in nearby Margaret Street.

The scene in 2010 is of the already outdated and outmoded Fletchers Walk and Birmingham School of Music. The subway under Paradise Circus was filled in April 2008 as part of a plan to extend the Midland Metro tram system from Snow Hill to Five Ways, but it now appears that the extension will only go as far as New Street Station.

AT THE OTHER end of Ratcliff Place, at the junction with Edmund Street, lay these two buildings. To the left, and continuing in the style of the Midland Institute, is the Central Library. The original library on this site was destroyed by fire in 1879 so, when the library was rebuilt, it was easy to design it to compliment its neighbour. To the right is what was originally created as Mason Science College. Founded by Josiah Mason in 1875 and opened in 1880, this institution would go on to form the basis of the University of Birmingham. The statue to the right of the library is that of Joseph Priestley. The windmill was a ticket office for the Tulip Festival that was held at Cannon Hill Park. In 2010 the area is occupied by the current Central Library, opened in 1974 and designed by John Madin. It is likely that demolition of this building will occur once the new Library of Birmingham opens in 2013.

THESE TWO VIEWS of the interior of the old Central Library give a real flavour of how attractive it was inside. Above we see the reading room. Note how crude the attempts to bring the building up to date are – with the ugly blue boxes providing either heating or air conditioning while the fluorescent strip lights must have created a poor substitute for the daylight that is flooding the room on the day this picture was taken. Below is the ornate splendour of the Shakespeare Memorial Room, designed by John Chamberlain in 1882. It is reassuring to know that this room was dismantled and rebuilt within the School of Music, a rare act considering what else was callously discarded. The library soldiered on as a lone survivor of Victorian Birmingham in this part of the city as it was slowly surrounded by 1970s concrete. Only when the contents were transferred to the new library would its days come to an end. It was finally demolished in October 1974.

THIS IS THE section of Great Charles Street that was lost when Paradise Circus was created. On the far right is the junction with Easy Row. The picture dates from the early 1960s and shows the scene shortly before demolition. For a time after, the site became a car park. In 2010 the site of these buildings is the corner of the Central Library building, seen below, and the rear of the Yardbird Jazz Club.

45

EASY ROW WAS a little bit of Georgian Birmingham that lay close to the city centre. The scene above from the early 1960s shows the section that lay between Great Charles Street and Edmund Street. The grand Victorian building of the National Savings bank had obviously replaced some earlier Georgian structures; it was originally built as the Birmingham & Midland Homoeopathic Hospital in 1873, a role it was still fulfilling as late as 1946. To the left is the shop of Thomas Smith, who made violins and cellos. Nearby Merry's are advertising 'Great Bargains' in their demolition sale. The scene in 2010 could not provide a greater contrast given the metal and glass that forms Chamberlain House offices. Easy Row disappeared from the map when Paradise Circus was created and Easy Row subway (which links Fletchers Walk to Alpha Tower) is all that is left to remind us of its existence today.

THIS MASSIVE BUILDING lay on Suffolk Street between Navigation Street and Swallow Street and had originally been opened in 1895 as the Municipal Technical School. Throughout its lifetime it would house the Central Technical College, Birmingham Central Grammar School and, finally, Matthew Boulton Technical College. This picture from around 1964 shows the building shortly before demolition. With a new Matthew Boulton Technical College premises opening on Sherlock Street and the Inner Ring Road soon to arrive at this part of the city, it was doomed. In 2010, the Brunel Street car park occupies the site.

THIS SCENE OF Thomas Gardens in the middle of Holloway Circus most likely dates to the latter half of 1966, as the mural that is attracting the interest of the photographer had been unveiled on 30 June 1966 by the Lord Mayor, Alderman H.E. Tyler. A plaque remains to tell that the mural, 'depicts activities in the Horse Fair which took place in this area until 1911 and was the last remaining fair of the charter granted by Henry III in 1215'. Of equal interest are the activities in the background. To the left are new factory and office units that have been built on Holloway Head, Blucher Street and Ellis Street. To the right, the old houses of Gough Street are awaiting demolition. The high quality of construction of the mural has resulted in it still looking good in 2010. The same can not be said of the buildings on Ellis Street!

A VIEW TAKEN from Horse Fair and dated 13 August 1955. The road to the left of centre is Suffolk Street, while John Bright Street can be seen on the right. Between the two lie the premises of publishers Newnes (who remain in business today). Above that is a prominent billboard for the Co-Op that informs us that CWS is the 'Sign of sound value at your Co-Operative store'. In 2010 this area is much changed. Only the building to the far right and Queens Gate offices on the corner of Suffolk Street Queensway and Severn Street indicate that this is indeed the same place.

THE FLEETING NATURE of any feature of Birmingham city centre is clearly illustrated by this picture of the site of the forthcoming Library of Birmingham, taken 21 April 2009. The sculpture in the foreground is 'Spirit & Enterprise', erected in 1991. The 'Flame of Hope', erected to celebrate the millennium, was extinguished due to a lack of funds. Both art works have since been removed as work on the library started at the end of 2009.

The new library is being constructed on the site of Cambridge Street car park that was located between Baskerville House and The Rep. Before work started, Birmingham Archaeology undertook an extensive investigation of the area.

Just below the surface they found extensive remains of Winfield's Brass Foundry which, in the mid-nineteenth century, was one of the largest brass works in the city and was well known for its brass bedsteads. These are some of the remains found.

AN AREA OF the city that has seen great changes in recent years is the part that surrounds the canals off Broad Street. Symphony Hall, the ICC, the NIA and Brindley Place are all relatively new, having been constructed within the last twenty-five years. Prior to these changes, much of the area was industrial. Above we see Tailby's Timber saw mill in around 1962. The canals were lined with premises like this but very few remain today. The scene in 2010 is similar only due to the layout of the canal and the cast-iron bridge that crosses it. The bridge includes in its casting a sign that dates it to 1827 and informs us that it was made at the Horseley Iron Works, Staffordshire. The large structure to the right is the National Indoor Arena, opened in 1991.

IT IS HARD to believe now but the area occupied by Symphony Hall and the ICC today was once a maze of small streets. This 1970s view shows Stratford House Antiques that stood at the junction of St Peter's Place and St Martin's Place. To the left the ornate railings and massive stonework mark the site of the Unitarian church of the Messiah that dated back to 1862. The church was constructed over the Worcester and Birmingham Canal but was sadly demolished in 1978. The view in 2010 shows that the site of Stratford House Antiques is now a service yard.

IN THE PICTURE above, at the end of St Peter's Place, a grand Georgian building in a state of semi-dereliction can just be seen. This building survives to this day and is known as The Brewmaster's House. Found just behind the ICC, it helps provide a real link with the past history of the area. A plaque located by the doorway and shown below provides some information on the history of the house.

By the 1980s, when developments in this area started, the council and the planners had realised that keeping some old buildings could actually enhance an area. Other notable survivors are Oozells Street School (now the Ikon Gallery), The Brasshouse and the Crown Inn.

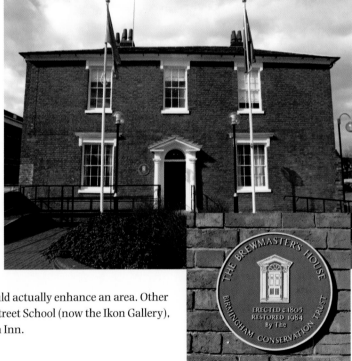

THIS EARLY 1960s view of the junction of Broad Street and Granville Street shows the factory premises of F&C Osler. In their prime Osler's were known for chandeliers and other light fittings. They famously provided the 8m tall crystal fountain for the Crystal Palace at the Great Exhibition of 1851. To the right is the home of Lee Longlands. This family firm first opened a shop on Broad Street in 1902 but the building seen both above and below dates from 1931 (as its Art Deco styling suggests). The Osler building was replaced by Granville House in around 1965, and in 2010 that building is now a Travelodge hotel.

THE END OF our journey brings us to Five Ways. The view above is from the early 1960s and shows the junction of Broad Street to the left with Islington Row to the right. The large building to the left of centre contained a branch of Kunzle's cafeterias, one of a number in the city. They were famed for their cakes, especially the Showboat! This area was demolished to make way for the Five Ways Shopping Centre and Auchinleck House that stands above it; these can be seen in the 2009 view below. In 2010 the shopping centre is awaiting redevelopment once again, the story of so many of the city's 1960s buildings. Five Ways roundabout was not completed until 1971.

3

PEDESTRIANISATION

A VIEW (CLEARLY from the early 1970s, given the way the lady to the right is dressed) showing the junction of Temple Row and Cherry Street shortly after pedestrianisation had been completed. The building behind the modern, sheltered benches was a branch of Midland Bank and has since been demolished.

In the 1950s the design of the Inner Ring Road scheme made it clear that the car was uppermost in the planners' minds. Numerous subways made this point clear, as pedestrians were forced underground at major road junctions.

Times change and by the 1970s the busy city-centre streets were not nice places to be. Cars and buses would block the progress of shoppers at every turn. Eventually the wisdom of pedestrianising the city centre became clear, and many areas were made totally traffic free. Of course, this was not just something that happened in Birmingham: town and city centres across the country were similarly redefined throughout the 1970s and 1980s.

Walking up the centre of New Street or High Street is something that we may take for granted today. It is hard to believe that such a thing was not possible just a few years ago.

TEMPLE ROW LOOKING towards the junction with Bull Street, *c.* 1972. In the distance is the popular Lewis's department store. The passageway under the store was known as The Minories and had originally been a road, so no doubt had to remain as a public right of way when Lewis's extended their store over the street in 1932. The company failed to keep up with the times and the store finally closed in 1991. In 2010 the former Lewis's building is now also known as The Minories.

TEMPLE ROW, AGAIN in around 1972, this time looking from Bull Street towards the site of St Philip's Cathedral. This time the sign of interest is the 'AMS' of Rackhams, another department store and a rival for nearby Lewis's. In 2010 the store is trading under the House of Fraser name and still operates a traditional department store format.

The Centrebus pulling out of Temple Row operated a route around the city centre for a flat fare of just two pence.

THE JUNCTION OF Temple Row and Cherry Street, *c.* 1972. Not only has this area since been pedestrianised but, in addition, every building visible in 1972 has been demolished and replaced. The need for pedestrianisation is clear as people and cars compete to make their way through the city centre.

THE OTHER END of Cherry Street at the junction with Corporation Street, *c.* 1972. The date of the pedestrianisation of Cherry Street was 2 October 1972, and it's clear that it was very much needed by this time. In 2010 Corporation Street is only open to buses, with private cars barred from using the road. The view below shows that a flower seller can now operate where once it was impossible. Also of note is how the cleaning of these buildings above shop-front level has had a dramatic result.

OPPOSITE THE JUNCTION of Cherry Street and Corporation Street is the junction with Union Street. As this view from 1972 shows, cars were also allowed to use this road, and negotiating the complex one-way system must have been quite a challenge for drivers!

THE PICTURE ABOVE is dated 28 November 1972, as are the remaining 'Then' pictures in this chapter, and shows Union Street looking towards the junction with High Street. Full pedestrianisation of Union Street did not come until the 1980s but the road was restricted to buses only earlier than this, as was High Street. The Marks & Spencer's store in the distance provides some continuity in the ever-changing city.

THE HIGH STREET, looking towards the junction with Union Street to the left and Carrs Lane to the right. It is clear that the pavement to the left has recently been widened as the road moves towards being used for buses only. Complete pedestrianisation would arrive in 1998 but, had it not come then, would have been forced upon the area anyway when construction of Bullring commenced in 2000 and all vehicular access to High Street disappeared for good.

THIS NOVEMBER 1972 picture of the junction of High Street and New Street captures 1970s Birmingham perfectly. From left to right we see one of the many subways that the city was well known for; in the distance the S&U building that stood in Edgbaston Street; the Bull Ring Shopping Centre; and, of course, the Rotunda. The contrast with the same scene in 2010 is dramatic indeed – and there is little doubt that the area is far more pedestrian friendly now than at any time since the car was invented!

4

LIVING IN THE CITY

HERE IS A familiar scene in Birmingham throughout the late 1950s, the 1960s and even into the early 1970s. Street after street of old houses were cleared to make way for modern replacements. This picture shows demolition in the Ladywood area.

In July 2004 a new attraction opened in the city centre. The National Trust back-to-backs were a great success, stirring memories for many and educating those too young to know such properties ever existed. It has often been said that it is amazing that the buildings survived, but when you consider that there were thousands of similar homes within a couple of miles of the city centre it is amazing they are the only survivors. The council practiced a wholesale slum-clearance programme throughout the 1950s and 1960s. A plan was put in place to create five new towns around the city. Some areas would simply be bulldozed and rebuilt, while others, such as Bath Row, would be renamed as well. In the process communities were destroyed, historic streets disappeared from the map of the city and hundreds of families were removed from their homes – all in the name of progress.

While it is true that most of what was demolished was lacking in the basics of modern life (such as indoor bathrooms), it is sad that much of what was built in its place was of poor quality and lasted for less time than the back-to-backs themselves. Indeed, by the 1990s residents were already proclaiming Lee Bank, formerly Bath Row, to once again be a slum. This led to a further phase of redevelopment and the area was renamed Attwood Green. Maybe this time the grand plans will be more successful? My visit to Attwood Green while working on this book has given me confidence that this will be the case.

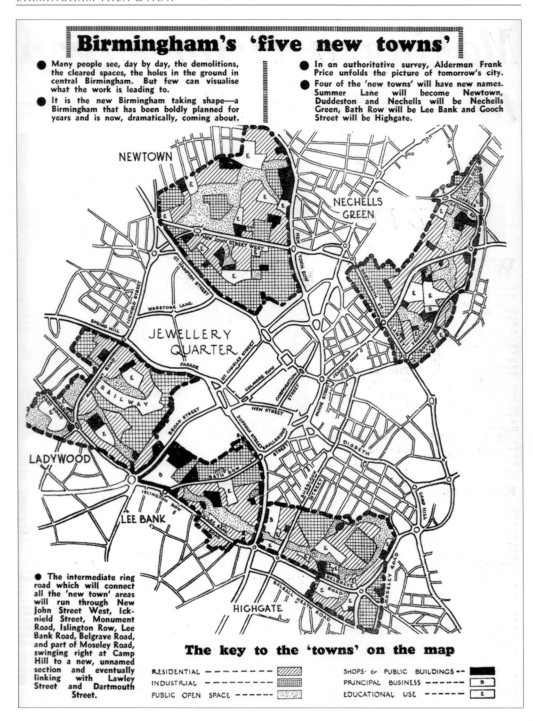

Birmingham's 'five new towns'

- Many people see, day by day, the demolitions, the cleared spaces, the holes in the ground in central Birmingham. But few can visualise what the work is leading to.
- It is the new Birmingham taking shape—a Birmingham that has been boldly planned for years and is now, dramatically, coming about.

- In an authoritative survey, Alderman Frank Price unfolds the picture of tomorrow's city.
- Four of the 'new towns' will have new names. Summer Lane will become Newtown, Duddeston and Nechells will be Nechells Green, Bath Row will be Lee Bank and Gooch Street will be Highgate.

- The intermediate ring road which will connect all the 'new town' areas will run through New John Street West, Icknield Street, Monument Road, Islington Row, Lee Bank Road, Belgrave Road, and part of Moseley Road, swinging right at Camp Hill to a new, unnamed section and eventually linking with Lawley Street and Dartmouth Street.

The key to the 'towns' on the map

RESIDENTIAL	▦	SHOPS & PUBLIC BUILDINGS	■
INDUSTRIAL	▦	PRINCIPAL BUSINESS	B
PUBLIC OPEN SPACE	░	EDUCATIONAL USE	E

ORIGINALLY PUBLISHED IN the *Birmingham Mail* sometime in the latter half of the 1950s, this was one of a number of articles written by Alderman Frank Price that was intended to keep the people of Birmingham informed about what was going on around them. The scale of the plan is dramatic. Five huge areas of the city would be pulled down and rebuilt. A new ring road would be created to link all the sites together. Residential and industrial sites would be separated and open spaces would be provided. It would be many years before the plan was fully implemented with work continuing right up to the early 1970s. (Reproduced by permission of Trinity Mirror Group)

BY THE EARLY 1960s, the master plan for the area north of Holloway Head (to make it largely industrial) was already taking shape. The junction of Holloway Head and Marshall Street shows many 1950s factories and offices with only the old Greyhound Inn providing a clue to how things used to be. At the top of Marshall Street the old houses in Upper Gough Street were yet to be demolished. By 2010 many of the industrial units had fallen out of use, the Greyhound was long gone and Midland Sandblast was a lap-dancing club! The final stage of the Mailbox scheme, The Cube, is well developed, and Upper Gough Street is now the site of modern apartments rather than crumbling terraces.

THESE BACK-TO-BACK houses, most likely dating back to the first half of the nineteenth century, were located on the north side of Latimer Street between the junctions with Great Colmore Street and Irving Street. Although the area was known for its poor housing conditions, it is clear that these well-dressed children are happy to be playing in the street and have no worries about the houses they are growing up in. Latimer Street was one of those whose name was wiped from the modern map; the closest point to the site of these houses in 2010 is the end of Lytham Croft.

BY THE LATE 1950s wholesale demolition of huge areas of the Lee Bank area were well underway. This view shows a site bounded by Great Colmore Street, Pigott Street, Latimer Street and Cregoe Street soon after demolition. The top half of Irving Street has been lost forever. The public house to the far right was the Shakespearian Bar. By 2010 the redevelopments of the 1960s had been swept away and replaced with modern apartment blocks.

ONE OF THE objectives of the plans for Birmingham's five new towns was to keep living and working premises a reasonable distance apart. This view, from around 1958, looks down the cobbled Speaking Stile Walk to the factory buildings very close to the houses of Irving Street seen in the distance. In 2010 the playing fields of St Thomas's School occupies this site with all traces of industry removed. The playing fields are under threat of being lost to further development in the area but local opposition is strong and the plans are being fought.

THE REMAINS OF St Thomas's church on Bath Row. The church, built in 1826, was bombed in 1940 but the classically styled tower somehow survived. To the left of the picture, from around 1961, is St Thomas's Infant School on the corner of Bath Row and Granville Street. In 2010 St Thomas's forms part of the Peace Gardens, also the home of an attractive colonnade moved from its original home in Broad Street in 1990.

THE COBBLED RYLAND Street, *c.* 1961. We have now moved to Ladywood, an area that saw great changes but at least kept its name. This view shows the part of the street that lay between Broad Street and Grosvenor Street West, roughly opposite Essington Street. One of the shops was a newsagent owned by J.A Turtle. Nearby was Mortimer Bros, who developed films. Behind these shops lay courts of back-to-back houses. To the left of the demolished building was the Ryland Arms. In the 2009 picture we see that this is now the site of The Square, a complex for small office-based businesses.

ANOTHER PHOTOGRAPH FROM around 1961 shows Joe's Cafe on the corner of Ryland Street and Grosvenor Street West. One of the hoardings says, 'Service, cleanliness and civility our motto'. The old buildings to the right still have the faded, painted signs of long-gone businesses. A pawnbroker proclaims that money will be advanced on such things as furniture, sewing machines and bicycles. On the far right the sign is for E.W. James, clothier. Ladywood is another area where the first generation of buildings erected to replace the back-to-backs have been demolished and replaced once more. In 2009 the scene is of yet more city-centre apartments.

A FINAL VIEW of Ryland Street, this time showing the great contrast that occurred as development progressed. In the distance is the newly built St John's Primary School. The grassed area in front of the school had been the site of two streets that disappeared from the map. These were Friston Street and Blythe Street and had been the site of many back-to-backs. A much older school, St Barnabas Elementary, is visible to the far right. In 2010, St John's remains but Ryland Street has changed dramatically with Callisto and Jupiter apartment blocks in place of the old shops and houses.

THIS PICTURE SHOWS one of the courts of back-to-back houses that existed between Morville Street and Blythe Street in around 1961. Accessed via a small alleyway and hemmed in by the blind back houses seen at the end of the court, it must have been a dark and damp environment. It is not surprising that the council saw total clearance of areas like this as the only sensible course of action.

A 1914 OS map and an aerial photograph of the area suggest that the most likely site of this court is, in 2010, the car park at the rear of Lincoln Tower.

BELOW WE SEE Monument Lane sidings as viewed from Monument Road in June 1955. To the right of the centre is the goods station. This was in the heart of Ladywood, and a smoky railway line and a busy siding was no obstacle to providing housing in the area. To the left are courts built between the houses of Shakespeare Road and the old Stour Valley line. This area to the north of the railway was very densely populated and many streets were completely removed during the 1960s. In the 2009 view from Ladywood Middleway, the sidings are long gone and the houses of St Marks Crescent are a healthy distance from the railway.

WHAT A FASCINATING scene... Mid-1960s in St Mark's Street, Ladywood, and all the generations are out on the street together. This is the kind of social interaction that was not possible in the tower blocks that were built to house many families from this area. At the end of the street is the building of John R. Lee, a firm of wallpaper wholesalers. The 2009 view shows that the line of modern-day St Marks Crescent does not match the old street, but the factory building ties the scenes together very well.

AN INTERESTING PAIR of pictures, taken from the top floor of Cambridge Tower, Ladywood. The view above is from around 1971, as that is close to the date that the Civic Centre development of four tower blocks was completed. The area close to the Birmingham and Fazeley Canal was largely industrial but many buildings in the streets to the south of Sand Pits, the curving road to the top right of the picture, have already been demolished by this time. In the view from 2009, industry has gone and offices and apartment blocks dominate the area.

This section of the canal network was one of the first to be enhanced as the city started to realise that the old canals could become an asset rather than a liability. Today Birmingham is well known for its canals and the towpaths are well used by its citizens.

THESE TWO VIEWS show either end of the stretch of New John Street West between Well Street and Wheeler Street. The premises of J.P. Lunt Ltd appear to pre-date the attractive cottages and almost look ready to fall down! Below is the Red House Inn, which had been in business since at least 1883. At the time the picture was taken (in around 1960) the landlord was George Arthur Powles. The yard to the left of the pub had originally been the site of ten back-to-backs and the bricked-up windows and doorways of some of them can just about be seen.

THE PICTURE ABOVE shows the junction of New John Street West and Great Russell Street, a stone's throw from the Red House Inn. The rebuilt frontage of the grocery shop is interesting. Could it have been the result of an accident or just an effort to modernise?

The streets to the north of New John Street West were swept away as part of the Five New Towns plan and, as seen below in the view from 2010, still form an area of 'public open space' as per that plan. The site of the Red House Inn now lies in the shadow of Geach and Rea tower blocks.

THIS PANORAMA FROM around 1964 shows the end of Alma Street, Aston, as it joins the Six Ways junction. The lady with a bike is standing outside Six Ways Post Office, while the shop in the centre has a prominent sign for a demolition sale.

On the other side of Alma Street to the shops shown in the panorama was the Alma Tavern. The pub occupied a site at the junction of Alma Street and High Street at Six Ways junction and dates back to at least 1860.

The road to the left of the Midland Bank building is Lozells Road while Birchfield Road disappears to the far right.

Although Aston wasn't part of the Five Towns plan, Six Ways was just on the edge of the Newtown area and all these buildings were demolished in the mid-1960s to make way for the Birchfield Road underpass seen in the 2010 view above.

THESE HOUSES WERE located on Ashted Row and dated back as far as the final years of the eighteenth century. It was at that time that the former estate of Dr John Ash was laid out for development and became known as Ashted. Pictured in around 1965, demolition would follow shortly after to make way for Nechells Green.

Below is a view of the rear of these properties from Willis Street and it is clear that the original blind back design was modified with numerous additions over the years. The array of chimneys is particularly interesting.

AT THE FAR end of the block, near the junction with Vauxhall Road, this house seems to have been better looked after than the rest. Even as late as the 1940s, this row of houses was occupied by surgeons, physicians and dentists. Maybe the resident of No. 101 was not willing to accept that the glory days of Ashted Row were long gone...

In 2010 the site of these houses is Hilden Road. The only indication that Ashted Row ever existed is the old street sign that still adorns the Dog and Partridge pub at the junction of Windsor Street and Nechells Parkway.

GREAT BROOK STREET was also part of the Ashted estate and these houses, located close to the junction with Vauxhall Road, would have been a similar age to those in Ashted Row. In this view from around 1965, the property closest to the camera was the home of the City Day Nursery. Ashted was originally a rather grand area, an attempt by the city to attract the merchant classes, but it fell out of favour in the latter half of the nineteenth-century as areas like Edgbaston were developed. Unlike Ashted, Edgbaston was not downwind of the city centre! A small portion of Great Brook Street does survive into the twenty-first century, close to Barrack Street. The modern picture, from 2010, shows that a small shopping centre now occupies the site of these once grand houses.

ANOTHER DEMOLITION site, this time Lupin Street in Nechells. To the left are houses in Willis Street awaiting the arrival of the bulldozer; in the centre is St Matthew's church and the familiar local site of a gasometer. The label for this picture identified this area as the, 'Site of Unit 6, Nechells', and a look at the next page will provide a clue to how that may have appeared. The picture from 2010 was taken from the junction of Wardlow Road and Duddeston Manor Road. The church is clearly visible but the gasometer is hidden behind the houses to the right.

THIS IS 'UNIT 11, Nechells Green', and captures the planner's view of the future all too clearly. The crudely constructed blocks of flats with their cold, Crittall metal windows and small balconies did not prove to be the great step forward from the back-to-backs that the council and the residents had hoped for. Socialising was difficult when there was no street frontage for all to share.

The communal play area that must have seemed a great idea on the drawing board quickly became outdated as the age of innocence passed. Who today would let their children play out unattended while watching them from four floors up? These blocks would disappear less than forty years after being built as people sought homes on a more human scale once again.

NAMED AFTER SIR Thomas Gooch, who owned large areas of land in Birmingham, Gooch Street stretched from Bromsgrove Street to Belgrave Road. It was surrounded by streets full of back-to-back houses and many of these were lost when the whole area was redeveloped as Highgate. Gooch St Garage was located on the stretch of the street between Wrentham Street and Sherlock Street, also lost during redevelopment. In 2010 Vernolds Croft occupies the missing section of Gooch Street.

THE 1960s REBUILDING of Highgate was not a new thing. In the late 1930s the city council had built St Martin's flats in an effort to improve conditions in the area. However, the poor-quality concrete used in their construction meant they quickly fell into a state of disrepair. They were finally demolished in the 1980s.

A huge area was cleared to make way for the flats but the council obviously didn't feel confident in knocking down the Emily Arms on the corner of Emily Street and Dymoke Street, as the early 1960s picture above shows! The picture from 2010 shows more conventional housing now occupies the area.

ANOTHER VIEW OF St Martin's flats, again in the early 1960s, from Vaughton Street (looking towards Vaughton Street South). The block on the right shows how much a coat of paint improves the appearance of the flats, but it can not stop the damp and the cold. The 2010 picture reveals that regular houses have replaced these outdated structures.

AN UNKNOWN PAIR of houses on an unknown street approaching the end of their useful life. The neighbouring property has already been abandoned, as have the upper floors of these houses. But the nets and curtains at the windows and the children's chalk marks on the walls show that, at the time, they were still homes to families – as they had been for many generations. The unusual alternating pattern of red and blue bricks suggests that these houses had been built with a sense of pride, maybe even an effort to impress. There is no doubt that many of the hundreds of houses demolished to make way for the Five New Towns plan were not acceptable for modern living, but many people feel that the loss of community that resulted was too high a price to pay.

BIRMINGHAM'S ONLY REMAINING back-to-back houses, located on the corner of Hurst Street and Inge Street, are now owned by the National Trust and open to the public. The picture above shows the Hurst Street properties that were built in 1831. Around the corner in Inge Street are several other houses dating back as far as 1821 that are available as holiday lets. The back-to-backs have become a popular attraction and pre-booking is essential.

AN ENTRANCE TO a time gone by... This gateway on Inge Street leads to Court 15, a fine example of the way so many citizens of Birmingham lived right up until the 1960s. Although criticised by some for being 'too posh', there is no doubt that these buildings are an important and fascinating reminder of the past.

BIBLIOGRAPHY

BOOKS

Baird, P., *The Bullring Birmingham* (Sutton: Stroud, 2004)

Harvey, D., *Birmingham Past & Present: The City Centre Volume 1* (Past & Present: Kettering, 2002)

Harvey, D., *Birmingham Past & Present: The City Centre Volume 2* (Past & Present: Kettering, 2003)

Line, P., *Birmingham: A History in Maps* (The History Press: Stroud, 2009)

Price, S., *Birmingham Old and New* (EP Publishing: Wakefield, 1981)

Skipp, V., *Victorian Birmingham* (Skipp: Birmingham, 1983)

Whybrow, J., *How Does Your Birmingham Grow?* (John Whybrow: Birmingham, 1972)

Whybrow, J. and Whitehouse, R., *How Birmingham Became a Great City* (John Whybrow: Birmingham, 1976)

OTHER SOURCES

Bartholomew's Pocket Atlas & Guide To Birmingham (Bartholomew: Edinburgh, 1945)

Kelly's *Directory of Birmingham and its Suburbs* 1883 and 1946 (CD editions)

The New Birmingham (The Birmingham Mail and Public Works Committee: Birmingham, undated)

Old Ordnance Survey Maps: Aston Manor 1913 (Alan Godfrey: Consett, 2007)

Old Ordnance Survey Maps: Central Birmingham 1902-11 (Alan Godfrey: Consett, 2003)

Old Ordnance Survey Maps: Birmingham North 1913 (Alan Godfrey: Consett, 2006)

Old Ordnance Survey Maps: Birmingham South 1913 (Alan Godfrey: Consett, 2005)

Old Ordnance Survey Maps: Birmingham West 1914 (Alan Godfrey: Consett, 2003)